AF229469

Perennials

POEMS BY DYLAH RAY

PERENNIALS

ISBN: 979-8-21834-950-9

For everyone who blooms,

despite all odds.

per·en·ni·al

/pəˈrenēəl/

Adjective

lasting or existing for a long or apparently infinite time; enduring or continually recurring

**"They thought they could bury us.
They didn't know we were seeds."**

I.

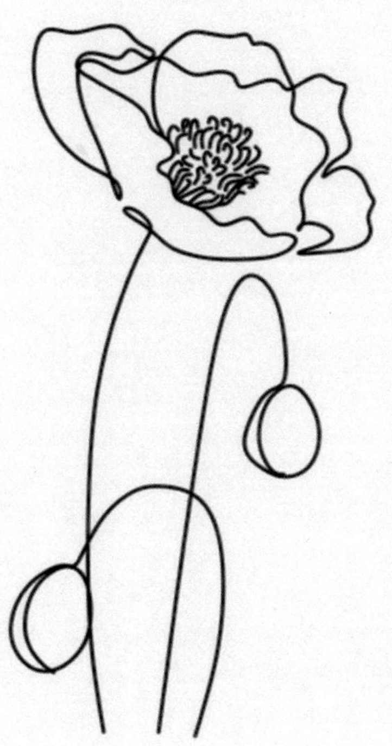

You made me prolific

I have written thousands of poems about you.
You don't deserve any of them,
and you deserve every last one.

Henry Street, Brooklyn Heights

I fell in love with you
in a sunbeam,
the best parts of you illuminated,
glowing with the heat and radiance
that only summer in a city of
endless tomorrows could bring.

I fell in love with you
surrounded by music.
Music you played, we danced to,
songs that will remind me of you, that you,
until my heart stops, until I'm dead.

I hope you remember
that there once was a time
I was desperate to know you
and feel you knowing me,
and to love you for every day of my life.

I will mourn for you,
the part of you that was light,
and curse the shadows that
stole away the beautiful boy

laying in a sunbeam
radiating my future.

Buy your own bandaids

It wasn't me you were trying to bury,
just the mirror I would not let fall from my hands.

Even as the glass shattered and the shards cut me open,
I held it steady.

That's how I ended up under layers of red clay
and volcanic ash and dirt.

You piled earth over me until I didn't know which way to dig,
if I should dig at all, or just succumb to the earth.

A fate I will certainly meet one day,
although it will not be soon.

It will not be because of you,
and I will not think of you as I go.

I will hold up my mirror every day until then.
You can turn away if you'd like,

but sirens will sound when you do.

If you plug your ears, I will write poems in a book
and rockets will fire with each turn of page,

writing our story across the sky for all to see;

And if I'm lucky, give you a paper cut
while you sit alone in an apartment

with no bandaids,
and no will to walk to the corner store, alone.

Have you heard of Maslow's hierarchy of needs?

This week, they say, after the incident, try to focus on

Safety
Security
Stability

such basic human needs,
but what do I know of them?

This is a task so enormous
so insurmountable,
my knees buckle
and I crumble into the dirt,
from which all things grow and return.

The most expensive cat bed (thoughts on marriage)

The cat has been sleeping curled up on my wedding dress
which fell off the hanger and crumpled onto itself
unable to withstand the enormity of its weight
giving up and surrendering to the ground.

I noticed when it fell six months ago.
I meant to pick it up but never got around to it
and now the cat has made the dress a bed,
his resting place after chasing birds and clawing furniture.

I certainly can't pick it up now,
it has only just begun to finally serve its purpose,
providing comfort, warmth, contentment.

Who would I be to take that away from the cat,
the only one of us who found a home
in that white dress.

You almost destroyed me

You almost destroyed me.

What a dangerous place
you now find yourself in,
because of that word, almost.

I am still alive and I am angry.

That is what I'd like to write,
But I cannot.

Because almost could just be
not quite yet.

There is plenty of time
for our mutual destruction,
and we're almost there.

The rebel

It's not lost on me that Leia's father becomes Darth Vader,
despite the attempts of her mother to keep him from the dark side.

His son will see good in him in the end
and try to save him, like his mother did before him.

How does the story change if there is no son?
and only the one rebel daughter?

The one who starts a princess, and ends a general.
Then what of his redemption?

Things I know to be true

It is possible to be in love
with more than one person at once,
and it is also possible to love no one at all.

It feels better to love
two people than to love no people.

Feeling lonely when you are alone
feels better than feeling lonely
when you are with people who
you can no longer love.

Hope strategy

I pull hope from my body like lambswool
willing each one to be long enough to lead me
in the right direction, to pull me towards
any place that isn't here.

But the yarn is knotted and tied up and
gets tangled
each time the weather turns cool
or Leonard Cohen comes on the radio
or that patriotic flag flies in the halls,
or the rainbow one doesn't.

But hope isn't a strategy,
I've recently learned
in my re-education.

Hope isn't blind.
It is carefully crafted,
curated around a collection of numbers and plans and people.
Hope is motivation for the masses,
but hope won't win the game.

Here I am all these years later,
holding onto it well past its expiration date,
grasping for possibilities that are impossible,
hoping that outcomes that are inevitable
will not come to be.

That maybe the lion chasing me will get tired,
and sit out the next lap.

But he has more resilience than hope,
hope like a flickering flame that only stays lit when fueled,
and is about to blow out.

One last storm

When the winter of all winters,
the one we could only endure because of the imminent spring,
finally ended with a whimper, waving a white flag,

trumpets blared, birds sang,
bees danced, victorious little soldiers finally returned home,
to seeds sprouting, buds blooming, tomatoes ripening.

When winter returned in surprise for one final battle,
snow more determined than before,
desperate to destroy
in the final moments of its relevance,
we were not ready.

The trees fell with remarkable speed
crushing the blossoming ground beneath them.
You could not help but look at the gardens and cry.

When the storm retreated, and we made our way back outside,
the sun shining on our faces, destruction at our feet,
we picked up our rakes, our shovels,
and began to tend to the earth once more,
as we always will, again and again and again.

The most expensive vet bill (thoughts on divorce)

There was no other option
besides the one that we chose,
and I would choose it again.

But now its Friday night,
and here I am
holding a dying animal
in my arms,
which is heartbreaking enough,

but the unbearable grief
is that I am alone,
trying to transfer
every ounce of comfort left in my body
to this miserable creature.

And while I do,
I'm watching a wife squeeze her husband's hand
as their dog gets out of surgery,
and a boyfriend wipe away tears from his partner's face,
when the news is not good.

I am alone in my grief,
drained of the comfort I need,
too wounded, too exhausted
to even look up
and try to find it.

Fragrant flowers and precious gemstones

I'm not the only one.

I have friends,

my women,

my worlds,

that have hearts and bodies

so bruised and mangled

that although they will be whole again,

their lives enveloped with light,

fragrant flowers and precious gemstones

filling in their footsteps as they walk,

not a day will pass where I don't tend to their wounds

and with every gentle touch,

think: revenge, revenge, revenge.

Not all men (but definitely you)

Not all men are bad, you said.
You offered yourself as a shining example
of what a man could be.

I recall I was not convinced by your argument,
that they weren't all so bad,
or that you were so good.

I was right on both counts, of course,
but there's still a chance I could be proven wrong
on one.

A meditation on all the assholes I've loved before (a lesson learned from my mother via Fiddler on the Roof)

I don't wish you suffering
but I am worthy of peace.

So the best I can offer you is this:
I wish you a lifetime of happiness,
far the fuck away from me.

II.

Ocean dip

Our obituary has been written
our caskets nailed shut
and buried on opposite ends of the world.

The mourners have come and gone,
but the death certificate, that decree which
matters in the eyes of god and country
has still not been delivered.

And when it comes, presumably in an email,
perhaps with the subject line, "divorce,"
and hopefully, if my lawyer would be so kind,
a little firework emoji,
where will I be?

Would it be too much to ask
to be on the beach,
on an island far from here?

And the very instant I see the divorce-emoji email,
drop my phone into the sand,
kick off my shoes,
run screaming with joy into the ocean

emerging triumphantly,
strong, refreshed, looking hot as hell
and ready to start life again with my feet firmly
planted on the sand?

It is a lot to ask,
but it is what I asked for,
and exactly what I got.

So, I'll just keep asking,
and building the life I want to live.
And next time I'm at the beach,
I won't think about you at all,
and my biggest concern will be
whether I put on enough sunscreen.

Happy Endings

I read books with unhappy endings,
poetry of love lost, faded on the page.

I want to take my place in the story of heartbreak,
so universally known, an earned sorrow.

But I don't miss you in the mornings,
don't ache for your body near mine.

The sound of your voice has left me
and I don't try to remember it.

I feel only redemption, cool grass on my toes,
sun on my shoulders,
bringing me back to life from the dead.

Nothing has inspired my creativity quite like your absence

Nothing has inspired my creativity
like your absence.

When you were here, I was a garden filled with weeds,
endless wishes wasted on dandelions.

Now that they've been pulled,
and you are gone,

dahlias and roses leap from the dirt
and the earth is filled with colors,

the sweetest strawberry sunrise,
that has never been seen before.

A love poem, for you

In my wildest fantasies,
it makes you sad to know that
I didn't write one love poem for you in ten years,
but I just filled a book with poems
that sing my joy
now that you are finally gone.

I write books now

Did you spend money buying my book,
the content of which I shared freely with you for a decade?
It turns out that a piece of blank paper
listens better than you.

Did you order it on Amazon,
too lazy and embarrassed to visit a store,

or am I still delivering you the sweetness
you can't create yourself,
dropping it off on your porch
paired with a perfectly baked pear pie,
the kind only I can make,
with a delicate lattice crust
and little purple pansies on top?

I can't wait to find out.

The joy of running out of words

The joy of sitting down
to write a poem,
and having one million thoughts
flood through my pen,
none of which are about you,
is unparalleled.

Up next

I can feel you
finally leaving me from my fingertips,
maybe just a few pages left
and then you will be gone.

There is a world
so much more beautiful than you
waiting to be written about,
and I can finally get started.

The birthday edition of Dante's Inferno

On my 34th birthday,
a friend gave me a gift,
and the gift was Dante's Inferno.

I think the friend could be more than a friend
but that would need to be in another life entirely,
on a planet roughly 1/8th as old as the universe and not 1/3rd
like the one we are on now.

He said, "this is your life - happy birthday dear."

In the crack of thunder that rose out of me,
that laugh from my belly,
dragged out kicking and screaming by the devil himself,
(who else could burrow so deep inside an earthly core),
I found joy.

You're the one I've been looking for

I have been turning over rocks on every beach I have been to,
on every continent I have explored,
looking for you.
I have searched for you in eyes that didn't see me
and tried to make people
without a fraction of your worth
become you,
when of course, they couldn't.

I've spent decades searching into the very depth
of my wildest dreams inventing you,
from the deepest desires of my soul,
only to have you stay right there.
And that's precisely where I finally found you,
the one I've been looking for: me.

We're learning

I don't need you
to hold me
in the dark
but when the light shines
over us at sunrise,
I want to share the same sunbeam
for a little longer.

Fresh strawberries

I know I should wait until after the last frost
to bury my seeds in the garden,
but I'm growing impatient to see new life
emerge from the ground in an exuberant dance.

And how do I know when the last frost
is the last frost anyway?
I've been wrong before
anticipating a new season
only to wake up to the same familiar blanket of white.

Everyone tells me I am starting too soon
and they will probably be right.
If you lean over the fence and hear me cursing the dirt
and my eternally misplaced optimism,
you will know they indeed were.

On the other hand, if your hear clinking glasses
and moans of delight
as the juice from ripe strawberries
drip down our faces,
you are welcome to come over
and lick the triumph off my lips.

Fall is for old flings

The golden leaves frame our hair
which after all of these years
still radiates warmth between us,
and down our cheeks
and still standing spines.

It's impossible to ignore the brightness
illuminating another life.
One where the distant past
and the pipe dream future is forever ablaze,
and a breathtaking honey
shines over everything we see.

I want to live in these golden weeks,
where bees rest on me like a sunflower,
where I become a sunflower,
and would become a hive, a home, if you asked me.

This world of gold where time stops
when we share the same hour,
and you brush my hair from my face
with such tenderness, I cry syrup.

But we should know better than this, and we do.
This place is too perfect, we agree.
Where is the darkness, the equal and opposite?
There would be no glow without it, so I know it's here,
under these bridges
overflowing with the seasonal splendor.

But for now, I'm going to keep my eyes pointed toward the sky,
letting myself stay drenched in the euphoria
of a rolling mountain of gold,
so fragile, it will disappear
with the next strong wind.

How it started/how it's going

Why is there something
about the muscles flexing
on the forearm of a douchebag
playing the guitar
that makes me want to put my brain
in a blender
and throw my clothes
on the microphone stand
that they think is still in front of them
even when they stop singing?

III.

Strangers

After Leonord Cohen

I sat alone in a crowded bar that was too loud and bright and too alive and dead at the same time, and I didn't want to be there, and I didn't want to be alone. So I took a long inhale to calm my nerves and watched a stranger across from me exhale it in relief. We locked eyes and giggled at our synchronicity. That stranger is still a stranger, but she didn't know who Leonard Cohen was, and she wanted me to write down some lyrics on a piece of paper for her, so I did. I hope she reads them and thinks of me and thinks of light. She's not wrong that our world is broken and we could fix it if we would, but we don't, and that's depressing as hell. But what about the way she rests her hand on her book, how her stomach moves when she laughs, her breath meets the steam on a cup of hot tea? How the light hits her just right to transform the shadows? This whole world is just one giant crack, but all I can see right now is the light pouring in.

What I mean when I text: hi, how're you?

For Tricia Fox

Thank you
for the 20 second hugs
and scientific explanation on why hugs need to be just so.

For the remedies
sharing your family, your healing.

For letting me cry in your arms
without warning.

For the nighttime drives
when yes, it's my fault I'm in this situation
but I still need help getting out of it.

For feeding me,
just like you do your own children,
even when i complain I can't eat,
just like your own children.

For mothering my daughter when I cannot,
for bringing her calm when there only is chaos.

For knowing the name of every single dinosaur,
and thinking that's just something everyone knows.

And most of all,
for the magic.
The inexplicable magic of not knowing me
and knowing me fully.

For loving me so that I feel it deep in my flesh,
when that's the only kind of love my flesh can handle.

For singing of sunshine, over and over again,
when I was standing in the rain.

For handing me a deck of cards,
where I pull "remember the good,"
although I didn't need a card to tell me,
because you've just come along to remind me,
that there is good here.

Right here.
And sometimes we just need to knock on our neighbor's door to find it.

Building a new world

After Mary Oliver
For Megan and for Leya

When my body couldn't carry you
And everyone and every cell
told me you wouldn't be,
I made you anyway, because
A new world needed building.

Hundreds of needles jabbed into my body
so I could draw you from my earth
to be grown by another woman,
the only woman to make me see god.

And now here you are,
My new universe, my holy of holies.
When I don't know which way is up
and what will be next,
you light the way as only you could,
my eternal flame through the darkness.

I read Mary Oliver over and over
and ignore her words pushing me
towards what I know is mine to take,
but there you are in the park,
chasing wild geese.

I give you paint and a brush and when
we do anything other than paint,
you yell "Art! Art! Art!,"

with such ferocity
it becomes a primal need,
one that I know.

I brought you here, and you deserve to know
that there is a safe path ahead of you,
that light will shine upon you, and
offer you a life of peace.

Although I wish I knew
if this world will be good to you,
I do not.

But what I do know is that
our lives will be precious,
our lives will be wild,
and we will fill them with the most beautiful
art we can create,
and we will do it together.

Knock first (The Botanical Bakery origin story)

My house is built from the kind of material
they don't make anymore,
the good stuff that lasts,
not like the cookie cutter homes
that fall apart if you just look at them hard enough.

My house is made with the most precious of corner stones,
stones that crossed oceans, that survived fire and floods,
that bore witness, were torn up and thrown out,
just to land here, the land of the living,
to hold up this house.

My house is made from the broken bones of women
who wanted to live, but who didn't,
women who left behind their bodies and their names
only in my body and in my name,
and demand each time I pick up a rolling pin,
that I use their bones for building.

My house has windows in every room,
letting in the warm breeze, and the moonlight
and the sounds of katydids announcing the arrival of summer.

My house has cracked open doors
that let in the cats with the missing ears
and the girls that want to kiss girls
and the teenagers that track in mud, not on their shoes
but on their bare feet and in between their toes.

My house has music seeping through the floorboards
and sliding down the stairwells,

and steeping in the chlorine.
As evening falls,
fireflies illuminate every corner of the house
and we get high on honeysuckle.

My house smells of baking bread
and if that weren't enough,
my house smells of cookies with a fragrant floral.

My house has protection painted on the front doorway
not from the blood of a lamb like in biblical times
but from the blood of the women
who believed the blood of the lamb would
protect them like in biblical times.

My house is built on a cemetery.
It holds the broken bones of my ancestors
and the growing bones of my children.
This is a house of life built on a solid foundation of death.
And that is why, when you come to my door, you must knock.

If you arrive with peace on your tongue,
you will be let in.
You will be let in to my house,
that I built,
on the bones on the women who came before me.

Who gave me my name,
who gave my daughter her name,
who whisper in my ear,
who use my hands to knead their dough.

I've been to the places they call holy

but let me tell you, nowhere is more holy than right here.

I will protect his house driven by the army of women who lie underneath it.

And if you threaten the sanctity of this place again,

I will bury you so far under ground,

in an unmarked grave, on a less desirable plot of land, far from here.

And when flowers finally start to make their way through the snow,

and grow by your headstone in the springtime,

I will pick them the first chance I get,

and bring them back to my house to eat every last one,

on top of a cookie so delicious, the foundation of my home rumbles

with delight.

I come from wildflowers

I know I come from wildflowers.
I knew it when I was sixteen and I sat down on a hillside
with flowers dancing in the summer sun,
and kissed each one of their petals,
the most delicate little triumphs,
growing on top of gas chambers.

I knew when I slept in fields of lavender
and then when I picked you up and ran
through valleys of burning poppies.

I dreamt of building a garden
that only the two of us could find,
and I did.

But how could I forget that I am from bluebonnets?
The one's my mother ran through,
that my grandmother planted,
that my great-grandmother carried over on a boat as seeds.

The ones that I cut down,
and you have never seen.

We come from bluebonnets,
and I didn't miss them
until it was too late for me
to find them.

Bone marrow

I thought we were at rock bottom,
the lowest of lows,
but now I've woken up to another shooting,
and see last week was just a pebble, floating among a sea of pebbles
all fragments of that bottom rock we hit long ago.

Two children survived.
They survived because they were protected.
Protected, underneath the bodies of their dead mothers.
And now I need to find my car keys and pack the lunch,
tie the shoes, get the image out of my head of my daughter's barely breath-
ing body
crushed under the weight of her dead mama.

So that I can smile.
So that I can be calm.
So that I can bring calm.

What I really need to do is bury my hands in dirt
submerge my body in water,
hold a newly born animal in my hands
to remember that we are still alive
that the people on this planet
still breathe and dream and glow.

That there is still good in our souls.
That there is still fire in our souls.
That we still have souls.

And when my hands dig into the earth,
I do remember and it's all I can remember.
I am filled with a primal thirst
to suck every drop of life from this place
and let it's dew revive me,
filling the ocean within me it's depleted.

I want to touch every blade of grass,
I want every ray of sun on my face,
I want to wear every color the eye can see.
I want to topple every dynasty,
I want to throw dishes, kick them, break them,
destroy them and repair them.

I want to kiss every person who wants to be kissed.
I want to burn this shit down and warm my friends with the flames.
I want to smash this glass earth into a million pieces
and build mosaics from it
that cannot be burned.

I will get cut up, but I will also take every ounce of joy
this decaying place can give me.

We're beneath the rock, we're deader than dead,
but I grew up watching women suck bone marrow
from dead animals,
and I became a gardener.

IV.

I've never been good at leaving

I stay and I stay,
until that tiny flame
finally catches and grows, and spreads through my veins
and fuels my soul and body

to run
climb
claw
fight
scream
Love

my way out.

Out.

I'm sorry for knowing myself, but deciding I didn't need to know more.
For choosing other people's happiness over my own.
For having one foot that wanted to dance
and one that wanted to march,
and for too often
letting the wrong foot lead.

Allegiances, a shift

After Emma Lazarus
For the queer community of Petals & Pages

I started pledging my allegiance to a flag before I knew how to tie my shoes, and so did you. My hand on my heart, I swore myself to this nation, and I meant it. I saw our flag wave in black and white on the moon and in vibrant color on my grandfather's lapel, which he wore every single day of his life, honoring the Mother of Exiles, who held her lamp beside the golden door, lighting the way for us.

I walked past one hundred and ninety three flags to get to my desk. Only one was mine, and I felt safety, pride, strength, and embarrassment all together all at once each time I walked by it. And when they gave me an American flag, paired with the one of peace on my last day, I was proud that I had represented my country well.

I've seen that flag plastered across ships carrying planes to drop bombs. I've walked through olive groves and picked up tear-gear canisters, and saw written on them what they wanted us to see written on them: Made in America. Respect our power, or our power will bring pain.

Once I carried red and green, instead of the white and blue that was expected of me, demanded of me. And when I did, I faced the metal of a gun and fists of rage. I was reminded of which flags hold power and what happens when power is confronted. I don't see blue and white without feeling the mouth of a gun on my hip. But I see those flags every day, in the places where I should pray, but can't pray, even when I want to, need to. I understand the power that waves through a flag, and so do you.

Whether you see a flag as a beacon of hope or strength or pain or isolation or exile or home, you know that a flag is never just a flag. But what you have underestimated, is that like all flags, this flag waves power too. Sure, it is dressed as a rainbow, and we don't stake it into the face of the moon. But this is a flag that radiates power, not by taking lives, but by saving them.

This flag wrapped me up, held my pain, spread it among its rainbow stripes, until what I carried was bearable. And then it continued to hold me: in kindness, in gentleness, in forgiveness, in gratitude, in all of my missteps and messiness, and then released me back into the world in a joyful exhale. I can't think of anything more powerful than being a life sustaining force on this dying earth.

I don't know what my grandfather would think about my Pride flag, and I'm not sure that it matters. But what I do know is that he wore his flag permanently pinned on his suit every day of his life, and I will wear my flag tattooed on my wrist for the rest of mine.

Although I thought I long lost my ability to pray, hear this prayer now:

God help you if you ever ask me to put down this flag again.

There are no pride flags in Paris

There are men sprawled across each other on benches
more entwined than the Rodin
that inspires them.

Women don't wear bras,
women kiss women, champagne drunk and unafraid,
standing under the soft street lights
that only brighten their glow.

They walk through old bookstores,
clasping hands and bouquets
walking home along the Seine,
arguing over which wine to open with dinner.

But where are the signs in the windows,
and in the front yards, and stores,
the flags, the waving colors that say:

you are safe here,
you can feel joy here,
we will let you be you here.

Do you know what it feels like
not wave pride from the rooftops?
To not shout the rainbow,
because no one is trying to take it from you?

Some people do, and may we all know it in our lifetimes.
Fow now, let our flags wave higher
until the day we pack them away,
not in hiding,
but in triumph.

An ode to the good men (why I only date women)

To the ones who want to make me theirs, but don't try,
who see me stretching toward the sun
and move out of the way so I can take in the light.

To the ones who see my roots growing stronger
and water the ground instead of pulling me up,
fearful that I will overtake the garden.

To the ones who admire me once I bloom,
tempted to put me in a vase,
but let me live and die on my own time:

You are the good men, and it's almost enough
to make me choose you, to come inside.
Spend my days indoors, on display,
in the perfect vintage vase
on clean granite countertops.

But as long as you're the one
who can pick up scissors,
and I'm the one who gets cut,
I'll choose a life in the dirt,
every time.

Open me carefully & I will be loud

After Emily Dickinson and Susan Huntington Gilbert Dickinson
For Catherine

How grateful I am that my love for you
is not confined to the page like theirs,
and I can shout it from tabletops
and blast it from the pixels on our phones.

My love for you will never be silent, restrained, or hidden.
I will love you with all of my being
and my being will be loud.

There will be no pretending or longing
and while we will certainly have friendship,
there will be no confusion about whether friendship
is the only kind of love that's ours.

You are the spring moon
that rose into my blackened sky,
showing me I still had stars.

You bring in a tide
that erodes footprints from past lifetimes.
And when you leave at night's end,
I long for the moon's gentle return.

That is to say, you have opened my heart
when I thought it could not be done,
and you have done so carefully.

And when they find our letters,
they will not be surprised.
Maybe they will put them in a bookstore
instead of burning them.

Ray's wedding dress covered in paint after a therapeutic session of artistic destruction with her girlfriend while listening to *Reputation* by Taylor Swift.

Photo Credit: Catherine Merritt

Acknowledgements

Thank you to my mom, who taught me strength.

To the poets of Denver, Colorado, particularly Sarah Herrin: Through your bravery and example, you convinced me to write again and it saved me. There is not enough gratitude in the world to convey how indebted I am to you.

Thank you to Beyond the Veil Press for publishing earlier versions of some of these poems.

In acknowledgement of my ex-husband, whom I've written dozens of poems about. You don't deserve any of them, and you deserve every last one.

Thank you to Taylor Swift for teaching me there is always another era on the horizon, and for *Reputation* and *Lover*, the albums that held me close during the writing of this book.

Thank you to Dianne for understanding and loving me fully, and for inspiring me to make my own art—it started with you.

This book would not have been possible without Catherine, my moon in the blackest night. Thank you for helping me shine along with you.

To my daughter, for making it all worth it.

DYLAH RAY is a queer poet and the owner of Petals & Pages, an independent bookstore in Denver, Colorado. Ray holds a BA from the University of Denver and an MA from Columbia University. *Perennials* is her first book.

Photo Credit: Kalli Wilkins